Young**Writers**

2004 POETRY COMPETITION

ONCE UPON A RHYME

IMAGINATION FOR
A NEW GENERATION

Flints~~hire~~

Steve Tw

GW00544284

 Young**Writers**

First published in Great Britain in 2004 by:
Young Writers
Remus House
Coltsfoot Drive
Peterborough
PE2 9JX
Telephone: 01733 890066
Website: www.youngwriters.co.uk

SB ISBN 1 84460 515 9

Foreword

Young Writers was established in 1991 and has been passionately devoted to the promotion of reading and writing in children and young adults ever since. The quest continues today. Young Writers remains as committed to engendering the fostering of burgeoning poetic and literary talent as ever.

This year's Young Writers competition has proven as vibrant and dynamic as ever and we are delighted to present a showcase of the best poetry from across the UK. Each poem has been carefully selected from a wealth of *Once Upon A Rhyme* entries before ultimately being published in this, our twelfth primary school poetry series.

Once again, we have been supremely impressed by the overall high quality of the entries we have received. The imagination, energy and creativity which has gone into each young writer's entry made choosing the best poems a challenging and often difficult but ultimately hugely rewarding task - the general high standard of the work submitted amply vindicating this opportunity to bring their poetry to a larger appreciative audience.

We sincerely hope you are pleased with our final selection and that you will enjoy *Once Upon A Rhyme Flintshire* for many years to come.

Contents

Toni Mason (10)	39
Siân Evans (10)	40
Elizabeth Stacey (10)	41
Chris Hall (10)	42
Jack Davies (10)	43
Sean Dunbar (9)	44
Alex Perkins (10)	45
Amy Blackwell (10)	46
Matthew Knobbs (10)	47
Heather Lambert (9)	48
Emma Griffiths (10)	49
Kayleigh (10)	50
Eleanor Douggie (10)	51
Ryan Jones (10)	52
Jack Higgott (10)	53
Gemma Watt (9)	54
Francesca Jones (9)	55
Amie Garratt (10)	56
Jessica Bremner (10)	57
Zoe Horswill (10)	58
Jake Higgins (9)	59
Laura Roberts (10)	60
Scott Pringle (9)	61
Bethanne Evans (10)	62
Daniel Lawton (10)	63
Joanna Waddy (10)	64
Emma Bircham (10)	65
Lauren Gillott (10)	66
Lyndon Williams (9)	67
Connor Jones (10)	68
Sophie Murray (9)	69
Jordan Ward (10)	70
Paul Harvey (10)	71
Charlotte Catton (10)	72
Ryan Parry (11)	73
Jack Lawrence (11)	74
Jordan Jenkins (11)	75
Jazz Beeston	76
Lisa Jones (11)	77
Stacey Aston (10)	78
Faye Bowers (11)	79
Nicole Murray (10)	80

Felicity Freeth   81
James Hughes (10)   82

Gwernymynydd CP School
Bethany Donkin (9)   83
Shannon Bonar (9)   84
Connie Roberts (7)   85
Liam Borthwick (7)   86
Ella Ramsay (7)   87
Kaylee Roberts (8)   88
Cara Maguire (8)   89
Abby Singleton (8)   90
Joseph Robinson (8)   91
Lee Jones (9)   92
Ricky Taylor (9)   93
Jack Campbell (8)   94
Leanne Williams (8)   95
Gareth Jones (8)   96
Emily Wynne-Jones (8)   97

Rhes-Y-Cae Primary School
Nathan Jones (9)   98
Sean Cullen (8)   99
Joshua Alton (9)   100
Ryan Thomas (10)   101
Robert Salisbury (10)   102
Gareth Roberts (10)   103
Philippa Jones (8)   104
Anna Hickie-Roberts (8)   105
Sara Denman (10)   106
Ffion Wright (7)   107

Westwood CP School
Nicholas Jones (10)   108
Stephanie Oldfield (9)   109
Shaun Tinsley (9)   110
Harry Wilton (9)   111
Andrew Cross (10)   112
Thomas Wright (9)   113
Hannah Taylor (10)   114

Sean Douglas (10)	152
Ruby Bamford (9)	153
Rhys Lewis (9)	154
Jessica Taylor (9)	155
Lewis Tattum (8)	156
Sophie Poscha (7)	157
Josie Ryder (8)	158
Molly Thomas (8)	159
Megan Roberts (7)	160
Leah Miles (8)	161
Catrin Barlow (7)	162
Rebecca Barnett (8)	163
Jack Connery (8)	164
Antonia Merry (8)	165
Amy Redding (8)	166
Siân Brisbane (7)	167
Daniel Smith (8)	168
Becky Morgan (9)	169
Nicole Connery (9)	170
Thomas Blackie (8)	171
Lydia Hughes (9)	172
Annah Hughes (8)	173
Georgia Brown (8)	174
Shannon Cameron (8)	175
Claudia Redding (8)	176
Emma Ley (8)	177

Ysgol Melyd Primary School

Conor Guthrie (10)	178

The Poems

The Enchanted Horse

(Based on 'The Enchanted Horse' by Magdelene Nabb)

In a cold, dark, frosty field
Pale moonlight reflecting
Footprints deep in the sparkling snow
Snowflakes falling heavily on the branches
Bella's breath steaming in the air.

Catherine Furness (7)
Custom House Lane Junior School

The Enchanted Horse

(Based on 'The Enchanted Horse' by Magdelene Nabb)

In a snowy, cold field
Moonlight reflecting on a frozen puddle
Snowflakes gently falling and twirling
Gently pulling down the dark branches
Footprints glittering down in the ice
Bella landed like a shield.

Jack Dunbar (8)
Custom House Lane Junior School

What Is A Scar?

A scar is a red dash
on a hurt face.

It is a black felt pen
lying on a peach floor.

It is a silver lolly stick
sitting in a dark bin.

It is a big pencil
waiting on a piece of paper.

It is a straight stick
worrying in a spooky forest.

Gemma Louise Jones (8)
Custom House Lane Junior School

The Enchanted Horse

(Based on 'The Enchanted Horse' by Magdelene Nabb)

A cold, dark, frosty night
Moonlight reflecting on an icy stream
Footprints deep down in the glittering snow
Snowflakes falling heavily on the branches
Bella's breath steaming.

Michael Jones-Williams (7)
Custom House Lane Junior School

The Enchanted Horse

(Based on 'The Enchanted Horse' by Magdelene Nabb)

In a cold, frosty night
The moonlight shining on the ice
Snowflakes drifting silently down
Footprints far away in the distance
Bella's mane swishing in the freezing air.

Amy Watt (7)
Custom House Lane Junior School

The Enchanted Horse

(Based on 'The Enchanted Horse' by Magdelene Nabb)

In a cold, dark, frosty field
Moonlight reflecting on a frozen stream
Footprints deep in the glittering ice
Snowflakes shining as they fall
Pulling down the frozen branches
The frost was like a giant shield
Protecting Bella.

William Sindall (7)
Custom House Lane Junior School

The Enchanted Horse

(Based on 'The Enchanted Horse' by Magdelene Nabb)

Shadows dart around
The moonlight reflecting on icy puddles
Snowflakes glittering on the branches
The dark, frosty field
She can see the snow in the distance.

Sarah Noble (8)
Custom House Lane Junior School

The Enchanted Horse

(Based on 'The Enchanted Horse' by Magdelene Nabb)

Far away in a frosty field
A frozen pond shines in the moonlight
Gentle snow patters on the ground
Sharp winds flying through the cold air
Hoof prints in the snow.

Matthew Genders (8)
Custom House Lane Junior School

The Enchanted Horse

(Based on 'The Enchanted Horse' by Magdelene Nabb)

Speeding through the icy field.
Panting, holding on to Bella's mane and tail.
Speeding like a falcon.
Galloping over the icy pond.
Flying in the dark, cloudy sky.

Sam Darbey (7)
Custom House Lane Junior School

The Enchanted Horse

(Based on 'The Enchanted Horse' by Magdelene Nabb)

Bella was charging across the dark field.
Swooping over the snowy gates.
Flying like a falcon.
All I could feel was the freezing air
And Bella's mane swishing.

Megan Cairney (7)
Custom House Lane Junior School

The Enchanted Horse

(Based on 'The Enchanted Horse' by Magdelene Nabb)

Speeding across the dark, icy field.
Flying like a falcon above the snowy ditches.
Bella panted, the breath steaming out of her mouth.
Grabbing tight onto Bella's mane.
We chased the snowflake field.
It made my heart beat fast.

Paige Garratt (7)
Custom House Lane Junior School

The Enchanted Horse

(Based on 'The Enchanted Horse' by Magdelene Nabb)

Charging across the freezing, dark field
Zooming like a falcon above the deadly ditches
Jumping over the highest branches
I was clinging onto Bella's boiling hot mane
Bella was like a gust of wind ripping through the night.

Nathan Roberts (7)
Custom House Lane Junior School

The Enchanted Horse

(Based on 'The Enchanted Horse' by Magdelene Nabb)

Charging across the dark, icy field
Flying like a falcon above the deadly ditches
Jumping across the stream that lay frozen in the field
Bella speeding across the snowy grass.

Tammy Massey
Custom House Lane Junior School

The Enchanted Horse

(Based on 'The Enchanted Horse' by Magdelene Nabb)

In a cold, frosty field
The moonlight reflected on the icy stream
Bella's mane blowing softly in the snow
Bella's footprints glittering deep down
The soft snowflakes pulling the branches down
Irina's dress sparkling in the dark night.

Amy Harley (8)
Custom House Lane Junior School

Street Man

On a freezing cold day
The street man
Trudges through the layers of snow,
Finding his way to the corner shop.
He clenches his jacket
As the strong winds compete with him,
Giving him goosebumps,
Making
His teeth chatter.

He can barely see a thing
Through the misty weather.
His mouth is dry and chapped,
And his skin is blue and frost-bitten.
The street is crowded,
And the man stays silent.
He dreams of a nice cup of tea,
In front of a blazing fire
On this freezing cold day.

Natalie Kelsall (10)
Custom House Lane Junior School

Street Man

The man always walks down our street
Bringing weather as cold as can be.
Freezing, foggy with a little snow,
He dreams of being in a nice warm bath
Or by a fire having a Sunday roast.
He always stands under that bus stop
With that old umbrella.

He passes groups of people
With laughter and with arguments.
He rubs his hands together
To keep them warm.
He decides to take a jog
To get to the old bin that he lays against.
His eyes are watering
His mouth dry and as stiff as can be
On this weak winter's day.

Ashley Marsh (10)
Custom House Lane Junior School

Street Man

On a freezing, snowy night
The street man
Wanders around lighting lights,
Wondering about the warmth.
He does up his jacket,
With the snow falling down on him
Continuously.
There is no shade
Apart from the houses he is gazing at.

His eyes start to water
While walking through the cold weather.
His mouth drooling while looking through windows.
Snow falls off his black hat onto his frost-bitten face.
This man is cold and alone.
He shouts but no one hears.
He dreams he is at home with a hot fire and a mug of cocoa
On this freezing cold night.

Chloe Pritchard (10)
Custom House Lane Junior School

The Street Man

On a foggy, windy day
the begging street man
crawls across the damp tiles
without direction,
he begs for food
as the rain beats fast
on him relentlessly.

His mouth opens for the rain
though everyone else is rushing around
he begs,
he shouts louder and louder
until someone throws a coin at him.
He goes silent as he runs to the nearest shop,
he buys a cheap bottle of water and a pasty,
he takes one bite,
a smile finally comes to his face.

Chantelle Johnson (10)
Custom House Lane Junior School

Street Man

On that busy street it's cold and rainy,
there is a man slowly walking,
he is looking at the ground, maybe his feet.
His skin is sore, cold and chapped,
his mouth is behind his red and white scarf,
his eyes are frozen and hurting with the cold.

The only shelter is the bus shelter,
his dreams are to be inside by a big log fire.
He walks on, listening to everyone around him
and rubbing himself to keep warm.
At last he turns the last corner and sees his house,
it was all glowing with warmness.

Billie Wibberley (10)
Custom House Lane Junior School

Street Man

On this icy, cold day
A helpless man
Sits outside a busy shop
Without money or a home.
He looks for something to put around him.
The frozen floor makes it worse for this man.
He is starting to get frostbite and it hurts him a lot,
There is no shade from this.

His mouth is hurting from asking people to help him
Through the bitter cold.
His eyes are tired and achy.
This man is homeless and cold.
No one will help him.
He asks for help
But no one listens.
He dreams of a nice hot drink and food in a house
On this icy, cold day.

Amy Hall (11)
Custom House Lane Junior School

Street Man

On a freezing cold day,
The lost man keeps on looking for a nice warm house
With a hot fireplace, but he does not know which direction.
He finds a woolly abandoned coat
And puts it on as there is no one in sight.

He finds it hard to see in the distance,
This man is alone,
He calls out but everyone is asleep.
He dreams of a hot drink,
And a nice warm bath on this freezing cold day.

Alistair Cairney (11)
Custom House Lane Junior School

Street Man

The old man shuffles slowly
Down the street
The pavements are dotted
With icy patches
The old man pulls his scruffy scarf
Tight around his neck

He looks for a place to shelter
From the cold, bitter wind
He dreams of a long night's sleep
In a comfy, warm bed
Of hot food and drinks
Just to be away from the
Cruel, cold climate.

Danny Femwick (11)
Custom House Lane Junior School

Street Man

On a freezing, snowy, winter's night,
When the moon is clear and bright.

A man walks down a busy high street,
He listens, he can hear muffled voices and lots of feet.

On this particular night he has a bad cold, so he puts his hand
in his pocket,
And from it pulls a Soother locket.

Over the road he sees a tramp lying on his tummy,
The man crosses over and in his hand he puts some money.

He dreams the tramp had a home tonight,
He wishes it with all his might.

He wishes he could give him a hot drink and food,
Someone to fuss over him and make him a cool dude.

The man then feels something fall on his shoulder,
So light and white like a speck of a boulder.

He looks up above, it's starting to snow,
Then he looks at the bags that he has to tow.

He makes a dash to the nearest bus stop,
The bags are so heavy he's starting to flop.

He catches the very last bus home,
Looks out the window, sees the snow looks like foam.

He thinks about what a great day he's had,
He then thinks of the tramp and feels mad.

He wishes that everyone had food, family and a home,
A nice garden with a cute little gnome.

Amy Hibberd (11)
Custom House Lane Junior School

Street Man

An old grey man staring,
stares into the open fire.
As he wonders about the storm outside,
he reads a book
and thinks to himself
that people live on the street.
If only he could share
what he had with the world
and now we enclose this open book
to people who read it in the future.

Ben Davies (11)
Custom House Lane Junior School

Street Man

On a freezing cold day
The homeless man
Wanders around the crowded street
Looking lost
He removes his hat
As the wind
Blows him
Powerfully.

He rubs his hands together
While he carries on into the distance
His eyes baggy
His face turns blue because he is so cold
He is crowded
He mutters to himself
He dreams of a warm home
And a sip of a hot drink
On a freezing cold day.

Amie Preece (10)
Custom House Lane Junior School

Street Man

On a cold, wintry day
None of the children are out to play
The cold, poor man stops to look through the bakery window
His eyes glistening at the wonderful sights
Many people pass him by
Shouting, mumbling, saying hi
Among the blurry sounds of this
The beggar pleads but only gets a snarl and a hiss
The poor old man can only dream
Of all those buns full of cream
Oh how he wishes the beggar wouldn't mourn
For his heart is broken as though stabbed by a thorn
His eyes were popping
When he was window shopping
As though the possessions were made from gold
'Alas,' he said, 'for I shall never be
A man who shouts with happiness and glee.'
Everything is covered with a layer of snow
But something on the ground begins to glow
The poor old man could not believe his eyes
For there before him was a winner's prize!
Was it foil or maybe even money?
Someone must have dropped whilst in a hurry
What is this thing? We cannot say
It might just give the game away
I think we'll save it for another day.

Lucy Martin (10)
Custom House Lane Junior School

Street Man

There he sits in his cardboard box
Creeping round like a fox
Running round street to street
Thinking of some juicy meat
There he sees a packet of crisps
Picks them up with his grubby mitts
Then he returns to his little shelter
Shares them with his dog, Delta.

Josh Williams (11)
Custom House Lane Junior School

Street Man

On a cold winter's day
The shivering man
Pushes his way through the strong wind
With goosebumps.
He pulls his jacket closer
As the heavy snow
Falls on him,
Freezing.
There is a bus stop ahead.

He tries to see into the houses,
Through the darkness.
His teeth chattering.
Big goosebumps shiver on his numb skin.
This man has nowhere to go.
He hears teenagers laugh as he passes.
He dreams of a nice warm fire
And a lovely cottage
On this cold winter's day.

Fiona Clarke (11)
Custom House Lane Junior School

Street Man

It's a cold, misty, winter's day,
Chester Streets are solid with ice.
Street man opens his hut in the park,
Ready for his long hours, dawn till dark.
Hoping, no tramps, no litter, no butts today,
But knowing he would have no job and no pay.
Slowly prodding through the park into town,
Skin feels tight, mouth so dry,
But eyes looking all around.
People passing, he nods with a smile,
A quiet hello, then head goes down,
Searching the streets.

Alice Davies (10)
Custom House Lane Junior School

Street Man

On a calm, cold and snowy night,
People pass and go,
No, but not this man,
This man sits on the pavement,
Begging, hands open.
He grabs his jacket,
And pulls it round him, tightly.
People go as if he's not there,
He coughs but nobody cares.

His eyes half open,
In the falling snow,
His lips ice-blue,
With cold,
Skin shivering to death.
He calls for a place to stay,
But they ignore.
He dreams of a warm home,
And a place to sleep in.

Paige Keenan (11)
Custom House Lane Junior School

The Enchanted Horse

(Based on 'The Enchanted Horse' by Magdelene Nabb)

Bella was sparkling in the moonlight
Her mane blew in the breezy air
She darted through fields
She ran faster than a train
Irina felt wonderful and amazed
Irina's hair was blowing in the cold, icy air
Bella was flying like clouds
She was drifting in mid-air
The snow was silvery-cream
Bella was shimmering in reflection of streams
The sparkly snowflakes fell down on to us
Bella ran faster than a motorbike
Bella ran faster than any horse
She felt ice-cold as the hurricane wind blew past
Bella leapt and jumped and flew like stars
Irina felt boiling as Bella ran faster and faster
As Bella sparkled she began to slow down
As Bella trotted towards the barn she sparkled the last time.

Samuel Hibberd (7)
Custom House Lane Junior School

Bella The Magical Horse

(Based on 'The Enchanted Horse' by Magdelene Nabb)

Bella got faster and faster
She glittered in the moonlight
She ran like the wind
Through snowy fields
Irina felt excited and delighted
Her hair blew in the wind
Happy to be with Bella
Zooming through the fields
Galloping faster than the strong wind
Jumping over fences and gates
Galloping home.

Ryan Lee Lewis (7)
Custom House Lane Junior School

The Enchanted Horse

(Based on 'The Enchanted Horse' by Magdelene Nabb)

Bella was staring at the bright moon,
Bella's mane was swaying from side to side,
The starlight gleamed straight into Bella's eyes,
She went through the snowy fields,
Bella's hooves were ever so silent,
Irina put her feet to Bella's warm side,
Galloping faster than a train,
Irina's hair was flowing faster than a stream,
Irina's sparkling eyes sparkled in the moonlight,
Irina's hair was sparkling,
The trees were whispering,
The breeze was blowing quietly,
Bella slowed down gently,
She trotted towards the barn,
The moonlight caught her eyes for the last time.

Laura Jones (8)
Custom House Lane Junior School

Bella The Magical Horse

(Based on 'The Enchanted Horse' by Magdelene Nabb)

Bella was glowing, Irina was wowing,
Bella was zooming, Irina was swaying,
Bella was trotting, Irina was curling,
Bella was racing, Irina's hair was blowing back.

Bella was jumping through the frosty fields,
Galloping like the wind,
Irina was sparkling in the moonlight,
Glittering like a star.

Jessica Bennett
Custom House Lane Junior School

The Enchanted Horse

(Based on 'The Enchanted Horse' by Magdelene Nabb)

Bella was glittering,
Swirling through the moonlight,
Jumping like the wind,
Trotting through snowy, frosty fields,
Irina felt delighted and excited,
Hair sparkling silver, blowing behind her,
Jumping over dark ditches,
Over slippery, icy hedges,
Over the farmyard gate,
And into the barn.

Alex Jones (8)
Custom House Lane Junior School

Bella The Magical Horse

(Based on 'The Enchanted Horse' by Magdelene Nabb)

Irina was so excited, she jumped out of bed,
the snow was falling,
falling in soft white flakes,
Bella was trotting in the snow,
Irina couldn't wait,
her stomach was rumbling and grumbling,
Bella went trotting over the snowy bridge,
trees were rocking side to side,
they rushed down the valley,
Irina had a picnic and ate it,
Bella was trotting softly under the moonlight.
It became night, they went to get some tea,
then they went home,
they got home and went into the barn.

Katie Flavin (8)
Custom House Lane Junior School

Irina's First Ride On Bella

(Based on 'The Enchanted Horse' by Magdelene Nabb)

Bella sparkled in the moonlight,
Galloping through the midnight air,
Bella ran like the freezing cold midnight wind,
Galloping over frosty, snowy, icy fields,
Irina felt very happy because she had a magical horse,
Her hair was blowing backwards,
As it shimmered in the moonlight,
Irina was delighted to have Bella,
Irina's silver, sparkly hair was blowing in the icy wind,
As it drifted around in the fog,
The snow was softly falling from the sky,
As it got nearer,
You could see that they were shaped like snowflakes,
Irina felt amazed and delighted,
Irina's sparkly, silvery hair was flying backwards,
Shining in the moonlight,
Irina wasn't afraid at all,
She didn't think of where Bella was taking her,
Irina and Bella were at the farmyard gate,
Where Irina tumbled off Bella's back,
'Goodnight, Bella,' said Irina.

Jessica Daltrey (7)
Custom House Lane Junior School

My Monster Poem

What does my monster look like?
My monster is kind of hairy
and really quite scary
and has a hedgehog's sting
and swan's wings.
That's what my monster looks like . . .

How does my monster move?
Well my monster waddles
and crawls and shuffles
and ambles and shambles
and sometimes scuffles.
That's how my monster moves . . .

How does my monster eat?
Well it slurps and burps
and nibbles and chews
and crunches and slurps
and eats my shoes.
That's how my monster eats . . .

What does my monster eat?
Well it eats slugs and bugs
and fish and squid
and puppy dogs' tails
and little kids.
That's what my monster eats . . .

Lucy Jones (10)
Custom House Lane Junior School

My Monster Poem

What does my monster look like?
Well, my monster's very vicious
and sometimes very suspicious,
he is very hairy
and always very scary.
That's what my monster looks like . . .

How does my monster move?
Well, it creeps and it leaps
and it scrambles and it shuffles,
it waddles and it toddles
and it oozes and after that it snoozes.
That's how my monster moves . . .

What does my monster eat?
Well, slugs, snails and puppy dogs' tails,
sisters and homework
and nasty bats
and horrible rats.
That's what my monster eats . . .

Toni Mason (10)
Custom House Lane Junior School

My Monster Poem

What does my monster look like?
My monster has a green face
Sharp claws on its feet
Dangling tail as a snake
That's what my monster looks like

How does my monster move?
My monster moves by crawling
It pounces and it jumps
It likes to slither and slide
And it likes to slump
That's how my monster moves.

Where does my monster live?
My monster lives in the garden shed
It breaks everything
Scares me when I'm in bed
Because it roars all night
That's where my monster lives.

What does my monster eat?
My monster eats bats and rats
Slimy slugs
And furry cats
It eats all day and all night
So that's what my monster eats.

Siân Evans (10)
Custom House Lane Junior School

My Monster Poem

What does my monster look like?
My monster has snake eyes,
And deadly sharp claws,
A lion's body and dragon wings,
And great big snapping jaws,
That's what my monster looks like . . .

Where does my monster live?
My monster lives in sewers,
He lives in ditches and beds,
Deserts and pipes and toilets,
Watch out, he'll scare you in bed,
That's where my monster lives . . .

How does my monster eat?
My monster scoffs and gobbles,
He crunches and slurps,
Nibbles and gulps,
And does smelly burps,
That's how my monster eats.

How does my monster move?
My monster tumbles and stomps,
He flutters and hops,
He lumbers and crawls,
He toddles and flops,
That's how my monster moves.

Elizabeth Stacey (10)
Custom House Lane Junior School

My Monster Poem

What does my monster look like?
My monster has 3 giant eyes,
It has scaly skin,
You'd better be wise or you're in for a surprise,
And in a race you'd never win,
That's what my monster looks like!

Where does my monster live?
Well . . . in ditches, in sheds,
Down plug holes,
In cellars, under beds,
And in holes, just like moles,
That's where my monster lives!

What does my monster eat?
It eats slugs and bats,
And stones and squids,
And mud and rats,
And bones and kids,
That's what my monster eats!

Chris Hall (10)
Custom House Lane Junior School

My Monster Poem

What does my monster look like?
My monster Is gruesome
It has bulls' horns and a Cyclops' head
And sharp teeth, spiders' legs
If you fall asleep you're dead
That's what my monster looks like

How does my monster move?
It runs very fast
And walks in slow motion
It rolls past
And silently stoles
That's how my monster moves.

Jack Davies (10)
Custom House Lane Junior School

My Monster Poem

What does my monster look like?
My monster has a hairy mane,
and big sharp lion claws,
human leg, and eagle wings,
and a lion's deadly jaws.
That's what my monster looks like.

What does my monster eat?
My monster eats spiders and teachers,
bugs, other monsters, living creatures,
slugs, stones, squids and bats,
blood, bones, kids and rats.
That's what my monster eats.

Where does my monster live?
My monster lives in cupboards,
and also in the floorboards,
it lives in a smelly cave,
and never has a shave.
That's where my monster lives.

How does my monster move?
My monster creeps and waddles,
but never shuffles or toddles,
it oozes, slouches, crawls and shambles,
trudges, flies and ambles.
That's how my monster moves.

Sean Dunbar (9)
Custom House Lane Junior School

My Monster Poem

What does my monster look like?
My monster has one big eye
he has a hideous head
tentacles and pincers
And he frightens me in bed,
that's what my monster looks like . . .
How does my monster move?
My monster likes to walk
he runs after his prey
he hides in the bushes
and can keep it up all day,
that's how my monster moves . . .
What does my monster eat?
My monster eats stupid heroes
and rebel soldiers too
if you think you're one of these
he'll probably eat you too,
that's what my monster eats . . .

Alex Perkins (10)
Custom House Lane Junior School

My Monster Poem

What does my monster look like?
My monster is all hairy
My monster has two heads
It is very scary
It is sometimes not
That is what my monster looks like . . .

How does my monster move?
My monster swiftly flies
It gallops and it sprints
It spies and it cries
It ambles and it creeps
That's how my monster moves . . .

Where does my monster live?
My monster lives in walls
And in toilet blocks
It lives in shopping malls
And in pyramids
That's where my monster lives . . .

Amy Blackwell (10)
Custom House Lane Junior School

My Monster Poem

What does my monster look like?
My monster is really cool
It has a really long tongue
One long tail
And if you're not careful it will bite you in the bum
That's what my monster looks like.

How does my monster move?
It slithers, it jumps
It flies around
And runs a mile
Until it falls to the ground
That's how my monster moves.

Where does my monster live?
My monster lives on an island
Under the sea
The only one who can control it
Just happens to be me.

What does my monster eat?
Well my monster eats slimy slugs
People's flesh
And even half price rugs
Or a kid or two
That's what my monster eats.

Matthew Knobbs (10)
Custom House Lane Junior School

My Monster Poem

What does my monster look like?
My monster has three eyes
It is very hairy
Has great snapping jaws
And is very, very scary
That is what my monster looks like.

How does my monster move?
My monster prowls and flies
And crawls around the floors
And jumps and runs fast
And crashes into doors
That is how my monster moves.

Where does my monster live?
In a shed
And under the ground
In cupboards
And under my bed
That is where my monster lives.

How does my monster eat?
It slurps
And sips
And it nibbles
And burps
That is how my monster eats.

Heather Lambert (9)
Custom House Lane Junior School

My Monster Poem

What does my monster look like?
My monster is terribly hairy
and is very, very naughty
he can be very scary
and needs to learn some manners.
That's what my monster looks like.

What does my monster eat?
My monster eats dripping blood
and stones and bones and bats
he stomps and chomps all day
and his favourite food is rats.
That's what my monster eats.

Where does my monster live?
My monster lives in my garden shed
and scares everyone to death
he lives in plug holes, attics and pipes
and has nasty breath.
That's where my monster lives.

How does my monster move?
My monster shambles and leans
he was taught to toddle
he used to creep and slouch
and also learnt to waddle.
That's how my monster moves.

Emma Griffiths (10)
Custom House Lane Junior School

My Monster Poem

What does my monster look like?
Well . . . scary
and nasty, naughty
plus very hairy
and warty
that's what my monster looks like.

How does my monster move?
It shambles
it crawls
it shuffles
then dodges you when you try and kill it
that's how my monster moves.

Where does my monster live?
Well . . . sheds
beds, ditches and streets
it hides in your cupboards so beware!
That's where my monster lives.

What does my monster eat?
It eats teachers
and squid, homework (of course)
and kids
it also eats bones
that's what my monster eats.

Kayleigh (10)
Custom House Lane Junior School

My Monster Poem

What does my monster look like?
Well . . . furry
and blurry
pimply and dimply, furry and curly
wrinkled and crinkled.
That's what my monster looks like.

How does my monster move?
It oozes and shambles
it crawls and it ambles
toddles and it waddles.
That's how my monster moves.

Where does my monster live?
Garden sheds, under beds
in a hole with a mole
in a flap with a cat
in mud with a slug
with a dog in the fog.
That's where my monster lives.

What does my monster eat?
Bugs and slugs
kids and squid
stones and bones.
That's what my monster eats.

Eleanor Douggie (10)
Custom House Lane Junior School

My Monster Poem

What does my monster look like?
Well . . . scary
and furry
and burly
and it weighs a ton
and three gruesome eyes
that's what my monster looks like.

Where does my monster live?
Well . . . in sheds
in sewers
in springy beds
in children's heads
that's where my monster lives.

What does my monster eat?
Well . . . mud
and adults
and blood
and bugs
and slugs and bats
with squelchy squid and noisy kids
that's what my monster eats.

Ryan Jones (10)
Custom House Lane Junior School

My Monster Poem

What does my monster look like?
My monster has an ant's body
A giant head
One big scary eye
And it gets you when in bed
That's what my monster looks like.

How does my monster move?
Well it crawls
It falls
It oozes, it waddles and it jumps
And lumbers
And it trumps
That's how my monster moves.

Where does my monster live?
Under beds
And hanging on pegs
In the sewer and in fewer garden sheds
That's where my monster lives.

What does my monster eat?
Well adults
And slugs
And bugs and rats
And bones with bats
That's what my monster eats.

Jack Higgott (10)
Custom House Lane Junior School

My Monster Poem

What does a monster look like?
My monster has snake's eyes
and deadly sharp claws
a lion's body, dragon's wings
and great big snapping jaws
that's what my monster looks like.

What does my monster look like?
My monster is very slimy
it has a gruesome head
a scorpion's sting, dragon's wings
it turns you to stone like dead
that's what my monster looks like.

Gemma Watt (9)
Custom House Lane Junior School

My Monster Poem

What does my monster look like?
My monster has a gruesome head
He is very naughty and warty
He sure has got gorilla's arms
And can be very sporty
That's what my monster looks like!

How does my monster move?
He creeps and ambles and shuffles
Oozes and skids on the floor
My monster slouches and trudges
And crashes into walls
That's how my monster moves!

Where does my monster live?
He lives in my pencil case
And sometimes in the fridge
In the hole in the wall
And I can never get to bed
That's where my monster lives!

What does my monster eat?
Stones and gravel and wheels from cars
Dogs and cats and chalk from school
Pens and pencils and all those things
That's what my monster eats!

Francesca Jones (9)
Custom House Lane Junior School

My Monster Poem

What does my monster look like?
My monster is very spotty
It has a warty head
It has a snotty nose
And it raises from the dead
That's what my monster looks like

Where does my monster live?
It lives in caves and graves
It lives in sheds
Even in fridges and bridges
And it might be under your bed
That's where my monster lives

How does my monster eat?
It slurps, it burps
It gobbles, it gulps
It sips, swallows and scoffs
It even stuffs itself
That's how my monster eats

How does my monster move?
My monster slouches down the hall
It always shambles
It never toddles or creeps
But it always, always ambles
That's how my monster moves.

Amie Garratt (10)
Custom House Lane Junior School

My Monster Poem

What does my monster look like?
My monster's very hairy
And it has a devil's horn
My monster's very mean
And I wish it wasn't born.
That's what my monster looks like.

Where does my monster live?
My monster lives somewhere magical
Maybe a page of a book
Maybe somewhere tragic
Or even a castle or shop.
That's where my monster lives.

What does my monster eat?
My monster eats slimy flesh
Eyeballs, heads and bones
It wants to eat children
And snatches them from homes.
That's what my monster eats.

How does my monster move?
It stomps and it ambles
And sometimes when it walks
It slowly, creepily shambles
My monster loves to stalk.
That's how my monster moves.

Jessica Bremner (10)
Custom House Lane Junior School

My Monster Poem

What does my monster look like?
My monster is hairy and scary
it has a hideous head
and it's dimply and pimply
and has furry legs.
That's what my monster looks like.

What does my monster eat?
My monster eats slugs and snails
squids and kids
small rats and cats
adults and teachers.
That's what my monster eats.

How does my monster move?
Well it oozes and it shambles
it crawls and it ambles
and it slouches and it shuffles
and toddles and waddles.
That's how my monster moves.

Where does my monster live?
It lives in sheds and beds
in tins and bins
beneath city streets
just under your feet.
That's where my monster lives.

Zoe Horswill (10)
Custom House Lane Junior School

Question Time

What does a monster look like?
Well . . . hairy
and furry
and warty
and naughty and wrinkled and crinkled
and pimpled!
That's what a monster looks like!

How does a monster move?
Well . . . it shambles
and crawls
and waddles
and slouches and trudges and lumbers!
That's how a monster moves!

Where does a monster live?
Wardrobes
and play holes
and ditches
and city streets
and under tables and under your feet!
That's where a monster lives!

What does a monster eat?
Kids' hair,
bats, rats,
chalk
and blood and bones and children's eyes and chicken's feet!
That's what a monster eats!

Jake Higgins (9)
Custom House Lane Junior School

Question Time

What does my monster eat?
My monster eats slugs and bugs
and human brains and flesh
he also eats melted eyeballs on toast.
That's what a monster eats!

Where does a monster live?
My monster lives under a rug
in a hat with a mat
he lives under beds
in sheds and . . . *in your room*.
That's where a monster lives!

How does a monster eat?
Well he slurps and burps and scoffs and dribbles.
That's how a monster eats!

Laura Roberts (10)
Custom House Lane Junior School

Question Time

What does a monster look like?
Well . . . ugly
and furry
and tall
and scary and hairy and naughty and fat and
pimply and wrinkled . . .
that's what a monster looks like.

How does a monster move?
It runs
it crawls
it hops and it twirls, it skids and slides and jumps
it bumps and toddles, it walks and waggles . . .
that's how a monster moves.

Where does a monster live?
In gardens
under houses
in garages, socks and dens
beneath wardrobes just under your feet . . .
that's where a monster lives.

How does a monster eat?
It gobbles and stirs, chews and swallows
it chucks and munches, it burps and it chops . . .
that's how a monster eats.

Scott Pringle (9)
Custom House Lane Junior School

My Monster Poem

Where does a monster live?
Well . . . it
lives in a waterfall
and in beds, in wardrobes, in sheds and
ditches and streets just under your feet.
That's where a monster lives.

What does a monster eat?
Well . . . it
eats slugs and bugs and bats
and rats and cats and stones and mud and
bones and blood and squids and kids.
That's what a monster eats.

How does a monster move?
Well . . . it
oozes and crawls
it slouches and
trudges and waddles and creeps and it toddles.
That's how a monster moves.

What does a monster eat?
Well . . . it
eats slugs and
bats and rats and
cats and stones and
mud and bones and blood
and squids and kids.
That's what a monster eats.

Bethanne Evans (10)
Custom House Lane Junior School

Monster Poem

What does a monster look like?
Well, freaky and naughty and furry
and really hairy and mean and horrible,
that's what a monster looks like.

How does a monster move?
It slides and glides and flies and climbs
and creeps and trudges and waddles,
that's how a monster moves.

Where does a monster live?
In walls and drawers and floors and
stairs and ceilings and boxes
and cupboards and books and plug sockets,
that's where a monster lives.

How does a monster eat?
It crunches and munches and gobbles
and chews and nibbles,
that's how a monster eats.

What does a monster eat?
Sofas and chairs and boxes and
computers and cupboards and clocks
and children. 'Yummy!'
That's what a monster eats.

Daniel Lawton (10)
Custom House Lane Junior School

Monster Poem

My monster eats,
Children's dimples,
Grown-ups' pimples,
Drugs and bugs,
Dogs' tails,
Big snails,
Bats, cats,
And big black rats.

My monster eats like this,
Slurping and burping,
Licks and picks,
He eats naughty boys,
And all their precious toys,
Rabbits' ears,
Half-eaten deer,
Pack of bees,
Big fat owls from trees.

My monster looks like this,
He is green,
Eyebrows like green beans,
And his hair is full of snakes,
His teeth are covered with chocolate and cakes,
Got tail like a foal,
His eyes looks like red-hot coal,
His kidney sticks out,
He has a pig-like snout.

Joanna Waddy (10)
Custom House Lane Junior School

Question Time

What does a monster look like?
Well . . . warty,
and crinkled,
and furry,
and naughty and pimply and wrinkled . . .
that's what a monster looks like.

How does a monster move?
It shambles,
and slouches,
and waddles and ambles and toddles and waddles . . .
that's how a monster moves.

Where does a monster live?
In sheds,
dark ditches,
and in scary streets,
under beds, in old, old wardrobes,
beneath city streets, just under your smelly feet . . .
that's where a monster lives.

Emma Bircham (10)
Custom House Lane Junior School

Question Time

What does a monster look like?
Well, pimply and dimply and warty and
naughty and wrinkled and crinkled and blurry
and furry and scary and hairy
that's what a monster looks like.

How does a monster move?
It wiggles, it cheeps, it toddles
and it lumbers and it ambles
and it shambles and oozes and slithers
that's how a monster moves.

Where does a monster live?
Well, it lives in my bedroom
in my wardrobe, under my bed
in my bathroom and in my garden shed
that's where a monster lives.

How does a monster eat?
Slurps and burps and munches
and crunches and nibbles and swallows
that's how a monster eats.

Lauren Gillott (10)
Custom House Lane Junior School

Monster Poem

What dooo a monster look like?
Well, hairy
scary
furry
blurry
wrinkly

How does a monster move?
It scrambles
shambles
crawls
creeps

Where does a monster live?
pits
plug holes
streets

How does a monster eat?
Slurps
burps
gulps
scoffs.

Lyndon Williams (9)
Custom House Lane Junior School

Question Time

What does a monster look like?
Well . . . hairy
and scary
and dirty
and green or blue and small or big
and wrinkled.
that's what a monster looks like.

What does a monster eat?
Snails and frogs and spiders and birds
and gold and things that live
under the ground and human flesh
and blood and fish heads.
That's what a monster eats.

Where does a monster live?
In gardens
under beds
in graveyards, another planet.
That's where a monster lives.

Connor Jones (10)
Custom House Lane Junior School

My Monster Poem

What does a monster look like?
Hairy and scary and fat or skinny
and burly and wrinkly
that's what a monster looks like.

How does a monster move?
Oozes and ambles
toddles and waddles and
shuffles and slouches
that's how a monster moves.

Where does a monster live?
Beds, sheds, wardrobes
and plug holes and alleys
that's where a monster lives.

How does a monster eat?
Slurps and burps and
munches and chews
and nibbles and swallows
that's how a monster eats.

Sophie Murray (9)
Custom House Lane Junior School

Question Time

What does a monster look like?
Warty,
dimply,
crinkled,
burly, hairy, scary.
That's what a monster looks like.

How does a monster move?
It crawls,
it waddles,
oozes, ambles, trudges.
That's how a monster moves.

Where does a monster live?
In sheds,
plug holes,
in ditches, under beds, in wardrobes.
That's where a monster lives.

How does a monster eat?
It burps,
gobbles,
gulps, sips, swallows and it munches.
That's how a monster eats.

What does a monster eat?
Bugs, slugs and drinks blood and mud and
eats bricks and mud.
That's what a monster eats.

Jordan Ward (10)
Custom House Lane Junior School

Street Man!

A cold, miserable night,
the poor homeless man
wobbles to his shelter with his only friend, *alcohol*.
He buries himself in an old torn coat and bin bags.

He dreams to have warmth with a loveable family.
His eyes water as the wind gets to them
as he thinks of his wonderful dreams
on a cold, miserable night.

Paul Harvey (10)
Custom House Lane Junior School

The Street

The street man peers
Inside house windows
In tattered clothes
On this winter's day
The rain and wind
Beat down on him relentlessly
He has bags under his eyes
And his lips have turned blue.

His only shelter is a doorstep
In a dark alley
He dreams of family and friends
And a home to go to
As he mumbles to himself
He thinks of where to go
But he does not know
On this winter's day.

Charlotte Catton (10)
Custom House Lane Junior School

Street Man

On a freezing cold winter's night is a
poor, lonely man with cuts on his face.
Drinking alcohol from a brown bag,
picking cigarette stubs off the snowy floor.
Holes in his jacket and the rest of his clothes.
Lying on a broken bench, in a lonely lane.

Shivering as the wind blows against him.
Confused as he walks, talking to himself
as he wishes to be with a family
by a scorching fire, with a cup of tea.
Falling over as he tries to walk.

Ryan Parry (11)
Custom House Lane Junior School

The Street Man

On a cold, bleak, winter's day
a hunched figure is sleeping on the pavement,
filthy, cold and hungry.
He dreams of sitting by the fireside,
smoking a *whole* cigar and sipping hot cocoa,
before having a hot bath and
snuggling into his comfortable, warm bed.
Feeling safe and secure,
his loving family by his side.

His dream is soon shattered
as an icy-cold raindrop mercilessly lands
on his dirt-ingrained forehead,
leaving a snail-like trail down to his nose.
He struggles to his feet,
muttering curses from his sore, chapped lips,
for he is back in reality.
He limps off down the street,
picking up cigarette stubs, clawing at the ground
with his grubby long fingernails.
He stops to drink the last dregs of cider
from a bottle which is wrapped in brown paper.
His sad, tired eyes searching for his lost dream.

Jack Lawrence (11)
Custom House Lane Junior School

Street Man

On a freezing night,
The lonely street man looked for somewhere to shelter.

Dreaming of a warm fire and a hot cup of tea,
Instead he was sleeping in a bus stop on a bench.

He put newspapers over his scraggy clothes
To keep himself warm.

As he tried to touch his hands together,
He could not feel his fingers or toes.

He scraped his face on a bin bag
He was using for a pillow.

Jordan Jenkins (11)
Custom House Lane Junior School

Street Man

The man walks, shivering and
barely able to move.
He dreams of a cup of tea
by a nice warm fire.
The only shelter is a bench
in the park.
His eyes are stinging and
his lips are blue.
He can only rely on a
bottle of whisky he
found in the park.
He is getting frostbite
and he can only just make it
to the bench in the park.
He collapses.

Jazz Beeston
Custom House Lane Junior School

The Street Man Poem

On a cold and frosty night
The street man
Wanders across the icy road
Without anyone else
To notice
Keeps on rubbing himself to keep warm
His skin is shivering and red
His mouth is chattering and blue
And his eyes are red and sore

He dreams of a fire, nice and warm
With a cup of tea
He only has a bench and a newspaper
In an alleyway for shelter
This man is confused
He is lonely
He is sad
He is cold
He is the street man.

Lisa Jones (11)
Custom House Lane Junior School

Street Man

On a freezing cold day
The terrified man
Wanders up and down the dark alleys
There's nobody around
He puts bin bags and jackets on
As the cold wind blows around
It blasts on his face relentlessly
There's lots of shade
His eyes shut in the cold
His lips turn blue
Beads of ice drop from his skin
This man is alone
He calls but people don't look
He dreams of a warm house
And a hot cup of cocoa
On a freezing cold day.

Stacey Aston (10)
Custom House Lane Junior School

Street Man

On a windy, snowy night,
a poor street boy lies,
lonely and freezing,
with no family or warmth,
he lies watching people in their homes,
he dreams of warmth and a family he once had,
lying by the trash bins in rags.

He has no feelings in his hands and feet,
he's wet and cold, the icy wind whips down the street,
he longs for sleep, but he's too cold,
he only has his quilt, that's too small,
as he eventually closes his eyes,
thought of a family locked inside.

Faye Bowers (11)
Custom House Lane Junior School

Street Man

On a freezing cold day
The confused man
Walks across the icy street
Without any family
He puts on another layer
As the beating rain
Slaps down on him
Relentlessly
There is nowhere to go.

He closes his eyes
His mouth is dripping wet
Blobs of rain drop on his face
The man is alone
He cries as people pass
He dreams for a nice hot drink
A chair in front of a fire
On a freezing cold day.

Nicole Murray (10)
Custom House Lane Junior School

Street Man

On a freezing cold day
The froozing man
Wanders across the street
Without anywhere to go
He puts on his jacket
As the icy blasts of wind
Shivers on his skin
Relentlessly
He shelters under a tree.

His eyes squint in the cold
Through the cold
His mouth is blue and chattering
The white frost bites his skin
This man is alone
He talks to himself
His dream to have a warm drink
And to be by a warm fire
On a freezing cold day.

Felicity Freeth
Custom House Lane Junior School

Street Man

On a freezing cold night
a dying man
wanders across the freezing floor
without distraction
he puts on his jacket
as cold rain
beats down on him
relentlessly
there is no shelter

His eyes change colour
through the cold air
his thought is sour
rain drips down on his face
this man is dying
he calls but no one hears him
he dreams of a warm house and a family
and some medicine to make him better.

James Hughes (10)
Custom House Lane Junior School

Clouds

A cloud is an enormous bouncy castle
for a beautiful angel's birthday party.

It is a million sticks of pink fluffy candyfloss
waiting to be feasted upon.

A cloud is a lazy giant's crimson pillow
waiting for his mighty head.

It is a hundred frothy bubbles
for God's large bubble bath.

A cloud is a warm, cosy bed
for all the creatures of the world to sleep upon.

Bethany Donkin (9)
Gwernymynydd CP School

Snowflakes

A snowflake is a fairy's wedding dress
fluttering from Heaven.

It is white tissue paper
cut by God to decorate His world.

A snowflake is a solid silver rose
dropped from an angel's golden bag.

It is threads of fine, sparkly silk
from a spider's web.

A snowflake is a portal
to an unknown world.

Shannon Bonar (9)
Gwernymynydd CP School

Clouds

A cloud is white, fluffy candyfloss
dazzling in the air.

It is a bunny, glittering, tall,
bouncing around in a beautiful garden.

A cloud is hundreds of bubbles
in a shell bath.

It is a bush
covered in sparkly snowflakes.

A cloud is white fur
fallen from an angel's sparkly dress.

Connie Roberts (7)
Gwernymynydd CP School

The Moon

The moon is a zooming blade
floating beyond the stars.

It is half a Jaffa Cake
that escaped the sky from Earth.

The moon is a hot pancake
that floated up to space.

It is a yellow banana
hovering in the night sky.

The moon is a golden plate
that's fallen from God's Sunday dinner.

Liam Borthwick (7)
Gwernymynydd CP School

Stars

A star is a shining sparkler
drawing in the night sky.

It is a glittery diamond
hovering in outer space.

A star is a dazzling light bulb
facing Earth.

It is a million fireflies
lighting the sky.

A star is a silver hedgehog
walking in space.

Ella Ramsay (7)
Gwernymynydd CP School

Planets

A planet is a fiery gob-stopper
fallen from an astronaut's lunch box.

It is a melting chocolate Button
falling from a spaceship.

A planet is an angel's CD
from her golden bedroom.

It is a silver diamond ring
dropped by a fairy from her pink purse.

A planet is a blue wooden eyeball
that fell from a giant's eye.

Kaylee Roberts (8)
Gwernymynydd CP School

Spiders' Webs

A web is a fairy's hammock
botween two ancient oak trees.

It is a thousand stepping stones
leading to a magical world.

A web is a delicate snowflake
fallen from Neptune.

It is a wizard's snow skirt
caught on a thorn.

A web is a baby's shawl
dangling from a golden peg.

Cara Maguire (8)
Gwernymynydd CP School

Clouds

A cloud is a glistening white fruit bush
waiting to be picked in God's garden.

It is an ice cream
melting in the blazing sunshine.

A cloud is Cara's curly hair
floating around an angel's bedroom.

It is pieces of cotton wool
a little girl was praying on.

A cloud is a fluffy cushion
of pink candyfloss.

Abby Singleton (8)
Gwernymynydd CP School

The Moon

The moon is a silver banana
fallen from a giant's pink lunch box.

It is a white football
kicked off a Martian's pitch.

The moon is a shiny bomb
ready to explode.

It is a bumpy cushion
that fell from a giant's bed.

The moon is a pitted button
from a green elf's coat.

Joseph Robinson (8)
Gwernymynydd CP School

Spiders' Webs

A web is a spinning hypnotiser
dangling from the sky.

It is a dazzling cloud
standing still.

A web is a climbing frame
for a little boy.

It is a piece of pink, glittering candyfloss
stuck to the wall.

A web is a sparkling plate
for a spider's dinner.

Lee Jones (9)
Gwernymynydd CP School

The Planets

A planet is a yellow golf ball
fallon from an alien's Spanish golf bag.

It's a giant's red eye
looking down on Earth.

A planet is a mini Frisbee
hovering around the sun.

It's an orange head
eating its way through a planet.

A planet is a spicy meatball
just fallen from a paper plate.

Ricky Taylor (9)
Gwernymynydd CP School

Clouds

A cloud is candyfloss
waiting to be eaten by a giant.

It is cotton wool
stuffed into a teddy bear.

A cloud is a woolly sheep
hovering in the sky.

It is God's hair
floating in outer space.

A cloud is a white bush
with lots of berries on it.

Jack Campbell (8)
Gwernymynydd CP School

Waterfall

A waterfall is a fairy's slide
in a dazzling garden.

It is a hot bath
floating in space.

A waterfall is a Martian's drink
fallen from his lunch box.

It is a snail's shiny, glittery track
in God's house.

A waterfall is a million teardrops
from God's face.

Leanne Williams (8)
Gwernymynydd CP School

Clouds

A cloud is a piece of candyfloss
floating in the air.

It is stones
hovering over the sky.

A cloud is God's beard
flying in the air.

It is a piece of white paper.

A cloud is a piece of bubble gum
fallen from a Martian's bag.

Gareth Jones (8)
Gwernymynydd CP School

Snowflakes

A snowflake is a glittering pear drop
floating to the ground.

It is a very pretty angel
dressed in white.

A snowflake is an ice star
sitting on a golden rose.

It is God's teardrop
fallen from the sky.

A snowflake is a scoop of ice cream
lying on the sparkling ground.

Emily Wynne-Jones (8)
Gwernymynydd CP School

Autumn Verse

The leaves show their colours of red, yellow and brown,
while the wind is soft the leaves flutter down.
The wind blows the leaves around and around,
when the wind is still they flutter to the ground.

In autumn there is bonfire night,
as huge rockets go up and set the sky alight.
Bonfire night is a beautiful sight,
as fireworks zoom up with a bang and give us a fright.

The clocks go back at exactly twelve in the morning,
at the time most of us are still snoring.
The days are much shorter for our play,
further we get into this period the more we lose of our day.

Hallowe'en is a scary sight,
when kids give people a scary fright.
When people are sitting down to eat,
trick or treaters come asking for a sweet.

Trees are bare,
with no leaves to spare.
Soon it will be cold with the winter breeze,
but now it is leaves falling off trees.

Nathan Jones (9)
Rhes-Y-Cae Primary School

Autumn Verse

The trees are blowing in the breeze,
The leaves are falling off the trees.
To the ground they flutter down,
Yes they flutter into town.
The squirrels scamper up and down the tree,
Collecting nuts for their tea.
The prickly hedgehog is preparing for his winter sleep,
Getting warm in his little heap.
November 5th is on its way,
Off we go to a firework display.
The rockets zoom into the sky,
Making a loud noise flying by.
A pumpkin face is for Hallowe'en,
Witches and goblins to be seen.
Wizards are casting nasty spells,
High up in their castle cells.

Sean Cullen (8)
Rhes-Y-Cae Primary School

Autumn Verse

Autumn time is here again,
the leaves are collecting in the lane.
Red, yellow, brown and green fall
without a sound,
making a crunchy and crispy ground.

The animals are busy preparing
for the winter sleep,
from the curled up dormice you'll
never hear a peep.

Screeching fireworks and orange flames
spark up high,
bangs and crashes fill the air
on bonfire night
but all the animals still sleep tight.

Out and about on Hallowe'en,
girls and boys trick or treat,
pumpkins lanterns and vampire teeth
open the door and give us a sweet.

Joshua Alton (9)
Rhes-Y-Cae Primary School

Autumn Verse

The leaves change colour to red, brown and yellow,
As they are falling in the meadow.
The leaves are blown by the autumn breeze,
Up and away from their trees.

Rockets go into flight,
Until they explode into a beautiful sight.
As the beautiful fire blazes,
Everyone's excitement raises.

On the eleventh of November it is remembrance,
So we think of those who died with a two minute silence.
We wear a poppy to help us remember,
On every eleventh hour of November.

On Hallowe'en children hope to get a tasty sweet,
By playing a game called 'trick or treat'.
As people dress up as ghosts or ghouls,
Then they run around acting as fools.

Ryan Thomas (10)
Rhes-Y-Cae Primary School

Autumn Verse

Autumn is when the leaves turn a golden brown,
And then they start to flutter down.
As they glide slowly off the trees,
Blown off by the gentle breeze.

The animals get ready to hibernate in November,
It is important to get ready for their deep slumber.
Hedgehogs and badgers, into bed they squeeze,
Before the winter freeze.

In autumn you have bonfire night,
When fireworks set the skies alight.
In every town you go to there will be a display,
The bonfire is started by burning sticks and hay.

On Hallowe'en, kids like to go trick or treat,
Hoping to get their favourite sweet.
In Transylvania, vampires are said to appear,
I hope they do not come over here.

On armistice day we honour the dead by going to the
cenotaph to pray,
A big thank you we want to say.
We wear a poppy to help remember,
What happened on the 11th of November.

Robert Salisbury (10)
Rhes-Y-Cae Primary School

Autumn Verse

Autumn is when the leaves fly off tho tree,
When the wind blows off the leaves,
Autumn time is here,
All the leaves we have to clear.

Fireworks explode in the sky,
Bursting into colour way up high,
Fireworks go blazing right up to space,
See the excitement on children's faces.

On Remembrance Sunday we pray,
To remember them that day,
On Remembrance Sunday,
We remember them,
Those who died in the wars,
For a just and honest cause.

Gareth Roberts (10)
Rhes-Y-Cae Primary School

Autumn Verse

The autumn wind is blowing and the leaves are falling down,
Golden colours on the crispy ground make a colourful gown.
Autumn starts in September and ends in late November.
People go trick or treating in the autumn because it is Hallowe'en,
Witches, wizards, goblins to be seen.

Bonfire night is a fabulous sight,
Exploding rockets give us a lot of light.
The fireworks zoom up in the sky,
Exploding stars way up high.

It is fun to jump in crunchy leaves,
Our thanks to the trees.
The trees are so bare,
They have nothing to wear.

Philippa Jones (8)
Rhes-Y-Cae Primary School

Autumn Verse

The autumn wind is blowing,
The beautiful leaves are falling.
The colours of red, yellow, green and brown,
Cover the streets in the town.

The animals are preparing for hibernation,
It makes us think of the wonderful creation.
Bonfire night gives them a scare,
This night they do not want to share.

As the nuts fall from the trees,
The squirrels come and collect them all.
They store them all away from sight,
Then when they wake they have a bite.

Anna Hickie-Roberts (8)
Rhes-Y-Cae Primary School

Autumn Verse

All the different colours light up the sky,
The fireworks screeching up so high,
Some are quiet but some are loud,
Exploding sparks as high as the cloud.

Autumn's here, the nights are dark,
No more playing in the park,
The leaves have fallen on the ground,
Colours of orange and red are all around.

Farmers harvest their fruit and veg,
Children picking blackberries from along the hedge,
This is the end of my autumn rhyme,
I'll see you next year at the same time.

Sara Denman (10)
Rhes-Y-Cae Primary School

Autumn Verse

The autumn wind is blowing,
The colours are changing,
The farmers are ploughing,
The fields are all bare,
Trees have nothing to wear.

Trick or treating for a sweet,
Dressing up as a witch,
Or a ghost or a monster,
The fireworks are bright,
Rockets are a night sight,
But they give us a fright.

On Remembrance Sunday,
We remember the people,
Who have died in wars.

Ffion Wright (7)
Rhes-Y-Cae Primary School

I Love You

Did you know that God above
carried you for me to love,
He picked you out from all the rest
because He knows I love you best,
if I go to Heaven and you're not there
I'll write your name on a golden stair,
for all to look and see just how
much you mean to me.

Nicholas Jones (10)
Westwood CP School

I Wish It Would Snow

The leaves are on the ground
The frost is all around
It is very crisp and white
And shines bright at night
But I wish it would snow
And on my sledge I would go.

Stephanie Oldfield (9)
Westwood CP School

Dogs

Barking and growling
They echo in the silence of night
They are your friend but a threat to the unwelcome
With their warm fur coat and tails wagging
We can watch them walking and running
On the frost-covered fields
Back in the safety of their own domain
They curl up contented, waiting
For the next day.

Shaun Tinsley (9)
Westwood CP School

My BMX

If I had a BMX
I could do some awesome tricks
I would build a really wicked ramp
Made out of wood and bricks.

Harry Wilton (9)
Westwood CP School

The Lion And The Mouse

I wish I could be a lion or a mouse.
As a lion I'd be too big to stay in my house.
I would walk outside and scare people away.
My friends would come around and play.
As a mouse I'd run around and eat cheese.
My mum wouldn't find me, I could hide with ease.

Andrew Cross (10)
Westwood CP School

School Dinners

School dinners are yuck,
I feel sorry for those who eat the old muck!
They make me feel sick,
John, get a bucket, quick, quick, I feel sick.

Thomas Wright (9)
Westwood CP School

Humpty Dumpty

Humpty Dumpty ate a big pie
He ate so much he started to cry
He whinged and whined
For such a long time
So he went to bed
But fell on the floor instead
He bumped his head
He cracked his leg
And now he looks like scrambled egg.

Hannah Taylor (10)
Westwood CP School

I Wish I Was A Bird

I wish I was a bird,
I could fly across the ocean,
I could fly country to country,
Me and my brother could go to visit America,
And play on all the rides,
I wish I could be a bird just one very last time.

Tyrone Holbrook-Harris (9)
Westwood CP School

Clouds

Clouds, what are they made of?
Clouds, what do they do?
I wish I could reach the clouds,
Do you?

Cloud, I think they're great,
Clouds, fluffy and soft,
I imagine they're angels' beds,
Or great big bubbles to pop.

Chantel Taylor (9)
Westwood CP School

My Best Mate

My best mate is great,
She loves to sing and dance,
Her last name is Prance,
But get this though,
I can't pronounce her name,
I try and try,
But it's like some silly game,
Then she tells me it's Donna.

Jessica Waterhouse (10)
Westwood CP School

Snow

It starts coming down very light,
And soon becomes very white,
As it gets thicker and thicker,
The lights begin to flicker,
It falls down on the ground,
And soon becomes a mound,
And then you find out you're snowed in.

Donna Wilbraham (9)
Westwood CP School

Fireworks

Fireworks are shiny.
Fireworks are bright.
Fireworks make big bangs and shining light.

Fireworks bang and crackle.
Fireworks bang at night.
If it's dark in the sky,
You will hear bangs tonight.

Adam Clare (10)
Westwood CP School

My Mum

Brilliant cooker,
Lovely looker,
Messy keeper,
Very good sleeper,
Is a borer,
And a snorer,
And that's the things
I love about my mum.

Danielle Dudley (9)
Westwood CP School

Slowly

Slowly the caterpillar crept onto land,
Slowly goat hair grows strand by strand,
Slowly the band will lose its fashion,
Slowly the love will lose its passion,
Slowly the animals begin to die,
Slowly the caterpillar learns to fly,
Slowly the sheep will eat the grass,
But most slowly of all is the way it grows back.

Risje Davies (10)
Westwood CP School

Red Is . . .

Red is the sunset
Shining onto the beach ball net.

It is the colour of a devil's horns,
All spiky and bright.

Red is the colour of a burning fire
With flames flicking on the blocks of coal

It is the colour of red wine
In glasses all tall and full.

Red is the colour of a rose
Planted in the mud.

Bethany Hibbert (10)
Ysgol-Y-Faenol

Black

Black is a shadow stalking you
Wherever you go.

It is the colour that
Witches use to disguise themselves.

Black is the colour
Of the moonless sky.

It is the cold
And gloomy night.

Black is a quiet monster
Never to show its face.

It is a dark
And spiteful colour.

James Heath (11)
Ysgol-Y-Faenol

What Is A Dolphin?

What is a dolphin?
A dolphin is a mammal that
Splashes about in seawater with its friends.

It's a good swimmer
That dives and bobs up and down.

A dolphin is a friendly creature
Sharing its happiness with us.

It stays under water for ages
Like a mermaid swimming about.

A dolphin is like a fish,
All soft and silky.

Nadine Marie Jones (10)
Ysgol-Y-Faenol

Orange Is . . .

Orange is a beautiful sunset
Balancing on the clear horizon.

It's a flame of a fire
Meeting with the misty smoke.

Orange is lava sliding down the side
Of a mountain and spitting out of the crater.

It's a slug moving slowly across the floor,
Like the sun moving in the sky.

Orange is sand, like a shower of
Burning rocks falling from the sky.

Harvey Williams (11)
Ysgol-Y-Faenol

The Sea Is . . .

The sea is a wild horse,
Giant and brown.
He trots through the waves
Which reach out to the world
Second by second.
The hooves clip and clop
On the stones, banging their shoes.
All around the oceans and the world
The sea gallops through the heavy winds.

Nathan Young (10)
Ysgol-Y-Faenol

The Life Of A Toad – Kenning

Short leaper,
Fly eater,
Good swimmer,
Insect killer,
Sun soaker,
Loud croaker,
Water drinker,
Quick thinker,
What am I . . . ?

Myles Halton (11)
Ysgol-Y-Faenol

A Muddy Pig

There was a pig that rolled in mud
And then he heard a very big thud.
He looked at the ground, it started to shake,
Don't worry, it was only a small earthquake!

Emily Jones (9)
Ysgol-Y-Faenol

My Brother – Kenning

Nose picker,
Dull thinker,
Not a bright spark,
Scared of the dark,
Daydreamer,
Girl screamer,
Book lover,
It is my brother.

Ryan Jones (10)
Ysgol-Y-Faenol

Red Is . . .

Red is danger
Waiting for innocent victims!

Red is love,
Bringing two people together.

Red is blood
Pouring out of somebody.

Red is a flame,
Flickering and dancing in the darkness.

Red is the devil,
Haunting people all the time!

Emily Billcliff (9)
Ysgol-Y-Faenol

Yellow Is . . .

Yellow is the colour of happiness,
A child on their birthday.

Yellow is the glowing sun,
Shining brightly in the cloudless sky.

Yellow is the colour of the sand,
As I build it into a sandcastle.

Yellow is the golden daffodil,
Standing proud in the sea of green.

Yellow is the pollen of the daisy,
The sun on a cloudy day.

Emma Naylor (11)
Ysgol-Y-Faenol

On An Island

I went to an island
And what do you think I found?
I found some treasure buried in the ground.
What do you think was in it?
Some silver and gold
And I went to touch it,
Then the warden said, 'Hold!'

Jordan Preston (9)
Ysgol-Y-Faenol

The Cat

There was a cat
Who lived in a hat,
Who sat on a mat.
He had a friend, Bat,
And the cat
Saw a fat rat,
And the cat
Ate the fat rat.

John Hennigan (10)
Ysgol-Y-Faenol

Red

Red is a rose blooming in the morning,
It is the colour of blood dripping from a body.
It is the colour of evil eyes looking for their victims.
Red is the sunset going down on a beautiful summer day,
It is the colour of a royal gown.

Bethan Williams (11)
Ysgol-Y-Faenol

White

White is the colour of a crisp snowflake
Floating down above an icy lake.

It is the colour of a dove
Gliding around, the symbol of love.

White is the colour of a fluffy cloud
Up in the sky, oh so proud.

It is the colour of glue
Sticking friendship together, me and you.

White is the colour of a fresh school shirt,
Extremely clean, not a lot of dirt.

Becky Scott (11)
Ysgol-Y-Faenol

What Is Black?

Black is death,
Lurking for innocent victims.

Black is pain and misery,
Haunting the midnight sky.

Black is the claws of a tree
Swaying from side to side.

Black is a witch's cauldron,
Surrounded with bats.

Black is a spider,
Creepy and frightful.

Black seeps into my brain
With a colourless mood.

Samantha Dyer (11)
Ysgol-Y-Faenol

Red Is . . .

Red is a sunset
Gleaming in the evening.

Red is Ysgol-Y-Faenol
Jumpers.

Red is the scorching flame
Burning logs.

Red is the Devil's eyes
With fire in them.

Red is blood,
Congealing on my dry skin.

Red is someone
When they are shy.

Daniel Price (11)
Ysgol-Y-Faenol

My Teacher, Miss R – Kenning

Red wine drinker,
Funny teacher,
Book reader,
TV hater,
Red pen owner,
Book marker,
Good runner,
Loud shouter.

Annie Sweetman (11)
Ysgol-Y-Faenol

What Is Yellow?

Yellow is a daffodil
Standing proud and tall.

It is the sun
In the inky-blue sky.

Yellow is a ball of wool
Being knocked around by a cat.

It is the colour
Of the eyes of a bat.

Yellow is a car's headlights
Being flashed in the dark.

Tania Burns (10)
Ysgol-Y-Faenol

Black

B lack are the shadows
L urking in the night sky.
A ir swift and sombre.
C aps of witches, torn and ripped,
K ids trick or treat.

Gareth Jones (10)
Ysgol-Y-Faenol

What Is Black?

Black is an alley
Where murders take place.

It is a bat
Screeching to find its way.

Black is a cauldron
With spells bubbling.

It is the plague
Wiping out anything in its path.

Black is a shadow
Scurrying in light.

Scott Bamber (10)
Ysgol-Y-Faenol

My Hamster – Kenning

Pellet pooher,
Carpet chewer,
Cat teaser,
Finger eater,
Slow drinker,
Bar swinger,
Not a dancer,
He's my hamster.

Katy Bennett (10)
Ysgol-Y-Faenol

My Wicked, Wonderful Family

My family are very weird,
All the men have a beard.
All the ladies are very nice,
Even though they make terrible rice.

My mum is really mad,
Her food is terribly bad,
She loves making sushi,
Even though it's a bit too juicy.

My dad is as nice as can be,
He's weird because he ate a flea.
My dad has also got a donkey,
But his legs are really, really, wonky.

My sister is very contrary,
Her hair is really curly.
She answers back to everything,
She really loves her singing.

My brother is a pain,
He's really very insane,
He's football mad,
And he's very, very bad.

My family are a pain,
But I love them all the same!

Elan Morris (9)
Ysgol-Y-Llys

Weird Animals

I have a dog that always goes to the bog,
I have a shark swimming in the dark,
I have a cat that scratches the mat.
I saw a monkey who was so funky,
I saw a cow doing a bow.
I have a snake that ate Blake.
I saw a parrot eating a carrot.
I have a rat that lives under the mat.
I saw a snake swimming in the lake,
I saw a fish throwing a dish.

Liam Small (9)
Ysgol-Y-Llys

Football

I always play in football,
No matter if it rains,
And when I get the ball,
I never see it again.

Time for a corner,
No matter if it rains,
I do a header
And we have lost the ball again.

I'm in goal,
No matter if it rains,
I play about
And then they score again.

And then they win the game.

Matthew Aaron Jones (10)
Ysgol-Y-Llys

Weird Animals

I saw a pig smoking a cig,
I saw a duck eating muck.

I saw a snake, it was a fake,
I saw a dog eating a frog.

I saw a rat, it looked like a cat,
I saw a cow, it said, 'Miaow'.

I saw a lizard, it looked like a wizard,
I saw a fox inside a box.

I saw a pheasant, it wasn't pleasant.
I saw a mouse as big as a house.

I saw a gorilla eating vanilla,
I saw a bull eating a gull.

Charles Blackie (10)
Ysgol-Y-Llys

The Seasons

Spring
Spring is about eating lots of Easter eggs,
Spring is about lots of lambs prancing about,
Spring is about all the flowers in the world,
Spring is my favourite season.

Summer
Summer is about playing outside,
Summer is about sun shining towards us,
Summer is about everyone loving it,
Sun shines and makes me happy.

Autumn
Autumn is great, it's all about leaves,
In the autumn the leaves fall off the trees.
Autumn's leaves are very crunchy,
Autumn is my favourite.

Winter
The winter is very cold,
In the winter it glows,
Snow everywhere,
It makes me happy.

Ellen Barlow (9)
Ysgol-Y-Llys

The Strange Farm

Pigs wear wigs, who knows what type,
I even saw a cow bow, who knows how?
I saw a shark in the park,
How did he get there?
I will never know.
There is a funky and funny frog,
It lives in a house, with what type of Barbies,
In what type of house, I will never want to know.

Nicole Lyne (9)
Ysgol-Y-Llys

My Weird Family

My family is very weird,
My dad has got a very big beard.
The girls are very nice,
And very good at making rice.

My aunty is called Ilain,
She really is a big pain,
But when I find the words to say,
I tell her what I think all day.

My mum likes to cook
And she has a very big book.
She likes to read my poems,
She likes to read my stories too.

My uncle has got a lizard,
It looks like a wizard.
He makes the worst spells
And he makes the worst smells.

No need to say more,
Just step inside the door!

Georgia Haddon (9)
Ysgol-Y-Llys

My Family's Bellies

My dad's belly is
Hairy and smelly.
My mum's belly
Is as lumpy as a giant jelly.
My nan's belly
Is as heavy as a wellie.
My grandad's belly
Is as jumpy as jelly.
My cousin's belly
Is floppy as jelly.
My uncle's belly
Is stinky and smelly.
My auntie's belly
Is floppy as jelly,
And my belly
Is just perfect.

Nia Butler (9)
Ysgol-Y-Llys

Nightmare

It's a really scary night
And I haven't got a light.
The ghosts give me a fright
And my cover's tucked in tight.

I hope this is a dream
Because I just might scream.
I want to dive into a stream,
Because that thing is mean.

I really miss my mother,
My father and my brother,
I try to hide under my cover,
I feel I might suffer.

I want to run away,
But that thing makes me stay.
I want to . . .
Phew! It's only a nightmare.

David Sturgess (10)
Ysgol-Y-Llys

My Friends

My friend Lucy is juicy,
My friend Kelly is smelly,
My friend Blake eats cakes,
My friend Sean eats popcorn,
My friend want a car to take me to the bar,
My friend Blake likes to bake,
My friend Mark likes to take me to the park.

Sean Douglas (10)
Ysgol-Y-Llys

My Family

My sister is called Jane,
She is a pain.
My brother Jack
Sleeps in a sack.
My dad is lazy
And is always crazy.
I live in a zoo
With my monkey too.
My aunty Mandy
Is very handy.
My aunty Jane
Hits me with a cane.
My uncle's belly
Is as lumpy as jelly.
And that is everyone,
So please tell me
About your family.

Ruby Bamford (9)
Ysgol-Y-Llys

It Was A Dark And Stormy Night

It was a dark and stormy night,
I had everything but a light.
It was snowing really bad,
I was feeling really sad.

I didn't like the rain,
I had a really terrible pain,
It was even worse with the snow,
I was feeling very low.

I thought about my brother Jack,
Until I ran into a bag pack.
I really wanted to scream,
But that thing is too mean.

I ran away quickly,
Ugh! That thing is so sickly.
That thing just missed me,
It was about to kick me.

Rhys Lewis (9)
Ysgol-Y-Llys

My Funny Relatives And Funny Friends

I have a friend that has a dog,
I wonder if she has a fog?
My other friend had lots of cats,
But her house is still full of rats!
I have an aunty that looks like a mouse
And she lives in a very big house.
My other aunty is called Jane,
And she hits her dog with a cane!

My sister is called Samantha,
And she has a pet panther.
My other sister is called Anita,
And she has a pet cheetah.
My aunty Pat as a cat,
And she's just bought a new mat.
My cousin Mia has a deer
And her dad drinks lots of beer!

Jessica Taylor (9)
Ysgol-Y-Llys

Winter And Autumn

Winter
Winter is cold and warm,
It tastes like warm soup
And a cup of tea.
It sounds like wind
Blowing the trees down.
It smells like the turkey is cooking, I'd say,
It makes me feel happy and funny.

Autumn
Autumn is cold,
It tastes like toast and bacon.
It sounds like the wind is blowing,
It smells like the potatoes are burning, I'd say,
It makes me feel cold and warm.

Lewis Tattum (8)
Ysgol-Y-Llys

Winter And Summer

Winter
Winter is cold and there are snowflakes
Dropping from the sky.
It smells like Christmas, I'd say.
It sounds like people playing in the snow,
It makes me feel very cold,
It tastes like ice down my throat.

Summer
Summer is very hot, the sky looks bright,
It smells like the sun is getting hot.
It sounds like people are sunbathing,
It makes me feel hot.
It tastes like hot chocolate going down my throat.

Sophie Poscha (7)
Ysgol-Y-Llys

Winter And Summer

Winter
Winter is white and very dark green,
It tastes like warm, warm soup with carrots.
It sounds like rain is falling down, I'd say,
It smells like a cold breeze,
It makes me feel very cold and shivery.

Summer
Summer is hot and sunny,
It tastes like ice cream and swimming,
It sounds like birds are singing, I'd say,
It smells like going on holidays.
It makes me feel nice and warm.

Josie Ryder (8)
Ysgol-Y-Llys

Winter And Summer

Winter
Winter is dark black and blue,
It tastes like hot chocolate and soup,
It sounds like people playing,
It smells like soup boiling, I'd say,
It makes me feel cosy and warm.

Summer
Summer is orange and yellow,
It tastes like hot dogs,
It sounds like people splashing in the water,
It smells like ice cream,
It makes me feel sweaty and flushed.

Molly Thomas (8)
Ysgol-Y-Llys

Winter

Winter is dark blue and very cold,
It tastes like hot chocolate running down my throat,
It sounds like the wind blowing very fast,
It smells like the turkey, I'd say, running down my throat,
It makes me feel happy and cold.

Megan Roberts (7)
Ysgol-Y-Llys

Winter And Summer

Winter
Winter is dark grey and black,
It tastes like hot soup and hot cocoa,
It sounds like snow twirling,
It smells like chocolate melting, I'd say,
It makes me feel scared and cold.

Summer
Summer is really yellow and orange,
It tastes like cold ice cream,
It sounds like people splashing in the sea,
It smells like a big Sunday dinner,
It makes me feel happy and hungry.

Leah Miles (8)
Ysgol-Y-Llys

Winter

Winter is white and dark grey,
It tastes like hot stew and bread,
It sounds like snow is calling,
It smells like Christmas is coming,
It makes me feel happy and excited.

Catrin Barlow (7)
Ysgol-Y-Llys

Winter And Summer

Winter
Winter is grey and black,
It tastes like hot milk and cookies,
It sounds like howling winds,
It smells like Sunday dinner, I'd say,
It makes me feel cold and dark.

Summer
Summer is bright blue and white,
It tastes like ice cream and hot dogs,
It sounds like people splashing,
It smells like popcorn popping, I'd say,
It makes me feel happy and bright.

Rebecca Barnett (8)
Ysgol-Y-Llys

Winter

Winter is dark blue and dark yellow,
It tastes like hot porridge and warm chocolate,
It sounds like the rain falling,
It looks like snowmen in bobble hats,
It smells like cookies with tea,
It makes me feel cold.

Jack Connery (8)
Ysgol-Y-Llys

Winter And Summer

Winter
Winter is dark blue and black,
It tastes like warm soup and hot chocolate,
It sounds like people sledging,
It smells like Christmas pudding, I'd say,
It makes me feel warm and cosy.

Summer
Summer is light blue and orange,
It tastes like ice cream,
It sounds like people splashing in water,
It smells like hot dogs,
It makes me feel sweaty and happy.

Antonia Merry (8)
Ysgol-Y-Llys

Winter

Winter is bright white and dark black,
It tastes like warm porridge and tea,
It sounds like a cold breeze going through my hair,
It smells like melted cream, I'd say,
It makes me feel Christmassy and warm.

Amy Redding (8)
Ysgol-Y-Llys

Winter And Summer

Winter
Winter is great, white and grey,
It tastes like soup and bread and butter,
It sounds like the winter breeze in your ear,
It smells like hot chocolate and biscuits, I'd say,
It makes me feel hot and cold.

Summer
Summer is a great orange and light blue,
It tastes like lemon zest and tomato,
It sounds like children panting,
It smells like fresh tomato, I'd say,
It makes me feel boiling.

Siân Brisbane (7)
Ysgol-Y-Llys

Mabel

There was a young girl called Mabel,
Whose legs were too skinny and unstable,
She loved to play football
And made a toy mole,
But still she lives under a table.

Daniel Smith (8)
Ysgol-Y-Llys

All About Me

When I was one, I fed a swan,
When I was two, people would say, 'Boo!'
When I was three, I sat under a tree,
When I was four, I kicked the door,
When I was five, I felt alive,
When I was six, I learnt to mix,
When I was seven, I felt like eleven,
When I was eight, I chose my mate,
And now I'm nine, I like to dine,
And I look forward to being ten.

Becky Morgan (9)
Ysgol-Y-Llys

The Zoo

One day a girl went to the zoo,
Who had nothing better to do,
She met a spider
Who was the size of a tiger,
And ended up crying in the loo.

Nicole Connery (9)
Ysgol-Y-Llys

All About Me

When I was one, I was named Tom,
When I was two, I ate a shoe,
When I was three, I climbed a tree,
When I was four, I wanted more,
When I was five, I was still alive,
When I was six, I had a Twix,
When I was seven, I thought I was eleven,
Now I'm eight, I've turned out great.

Thomas Blackie (8)
Ysgol-Y-Llys

Mabel

There was a young girl called Mabel,
Who always set the table,
It always was messy,
She's always dressy,
And never went into the stable.

Lydia Hughes (9)
Ysgol-Y-Llys

Emotion

Grumpy is grey like a big, fat elephant,
It tastes like sloppy, lumpy mud,
It smells like a rotten egg.
It looks like an enormous toffee monster,
It sounds like a rumbling belly,
It feels like mushy peas.

Happy is funny, like Jumpy monkey in a zoo,
It tastes like nice red strawberries,
It smells like a big red rose in a garden,
It looks like happy children playing outside,
It sounds like birds singing up high,
It feels like fresh fruit salad.

Annah Hughes (8)
Ysgol-Y-Llys

Emotion Poem

Mad is red like a big unhappy dragon,
It tastes like green, sloppy peas,
It smells like a garbage bin that's smelly,
It looks like hot boiling lava,
It sounds like Dad in a bad mood,
It feels like ten freezing cold ice cubes.

Georgia Brown (8)
Ysgol-Y-Llys

Emotion

Grumpy is grey like a big, fat elephant,
It tastes like sloppy, lumpy mud,
It smells like a rotten egg,
It looks like an enormous toffee monster,
It sounds like a rumbling belly,
It feels like squashy bananas.

Happy is pink like a butterfly on a flower,
It tastes like lovely grapes,
It smells like delicious ice cream,
It looks like flowers growing,
It sounds like perfume dropping,
It feels like strawberries melting.

Shannon Cameron (8)
Ysgol-Y-Llys

Emotions

Happy
Happy is blue like the sea,
It tastes like a mint ice cream,
It smells like the salty water,
It looks like the hot sun,
It sounds like the birds singing,
It feels like we're playing.

Grumpy
Grumpy is grey like a big, fat elephant,
It tastes like sloppy, lumpy mud,
It smells like a rotten egg,
It looks like an enormous toffee monster,
It sounds like a rumbling belly,
It feels like a slimy slug.

Claudia Redding (8)
Ysgol-Y-Llys

Emotions

Grumpy
Grumpy is grey like a big, fat elephant,
It tastes like sloppy, lumpy mud,
It smells like a rotten egg,
It looks like an enormous toffee monster,
It sounds like a rumbling belly,
It feels like squashed tomatoes.

Happy
Happy is like the sun,
It tastes like a beautiful flower,
It smells like a gorgeous bar of chocolate,
It looks like a butterfly,
It sounds like a bird singing,
It feels like cuddling a teddy.

Emma Ley (8)
Ysgol-Y-Llys

Raindrops

R aindrops fall and splash on the ground noisily,
A nd rain trickles down gutters and off roofs,
I know, but do you?
N ow it's time to watch,
D rip, drop, drip, drop,
R ain falls like bricks from the sky so people take shelter,
O pen the window and you will hear a noise go drip, drop,
P eace may come with the sound of rain - a silent time to think.
S o go to a chair and listen for the sound.

Conor Guthrie (10)
Ysgol Melyd Primary School